Maths
made easy

Key Stage 1
ages 6-7
Beginner

Author
Sue Phillips

Consultant
Sean McArdle

LONDON • NEW YORK • MUNICH • MELBOURNE • DELHI

Numbers

Which numbers are the snakes hiding?
Look, and say them as you write.

1	2	3	4	5		7	8		
11			14	15		17		19	20
21	22		24	25		27	28		30
	32	33	34	35		37	38		
41			44	45	46			49	50

9 10

Calculators

Look at the keys on the calculator.
Colour the light bars for each number.

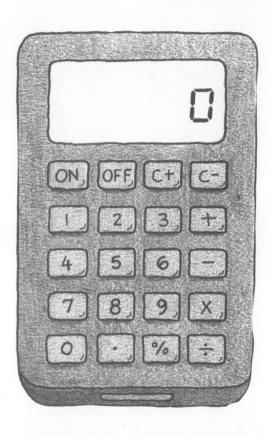

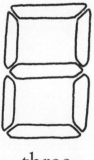

one

two

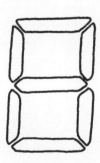

three

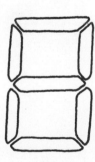

four

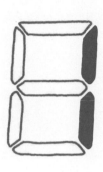

five

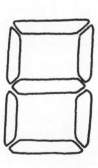

six

seven

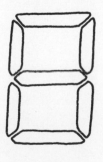

eight

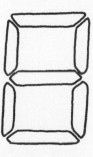

nine

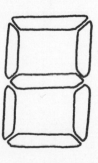

zero

1 less or 1 more

Count, draw and write.

1 less

55

1 less

56

1 more

57

1 more

54

58

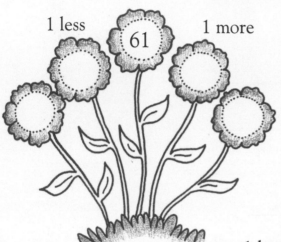

1 less

61

1 more

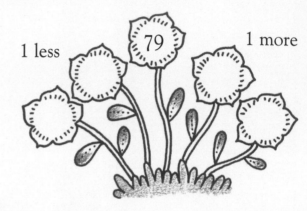

1 less

79

1 more

1 less

98

1 more

1 less

17

1 more

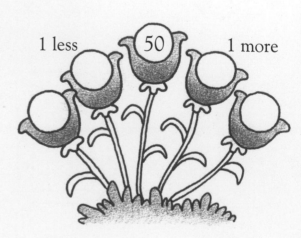

1 less

50

1 more

Counting in 2s

Draw in the hops and write in the numbers.
Do you need to add or take away?

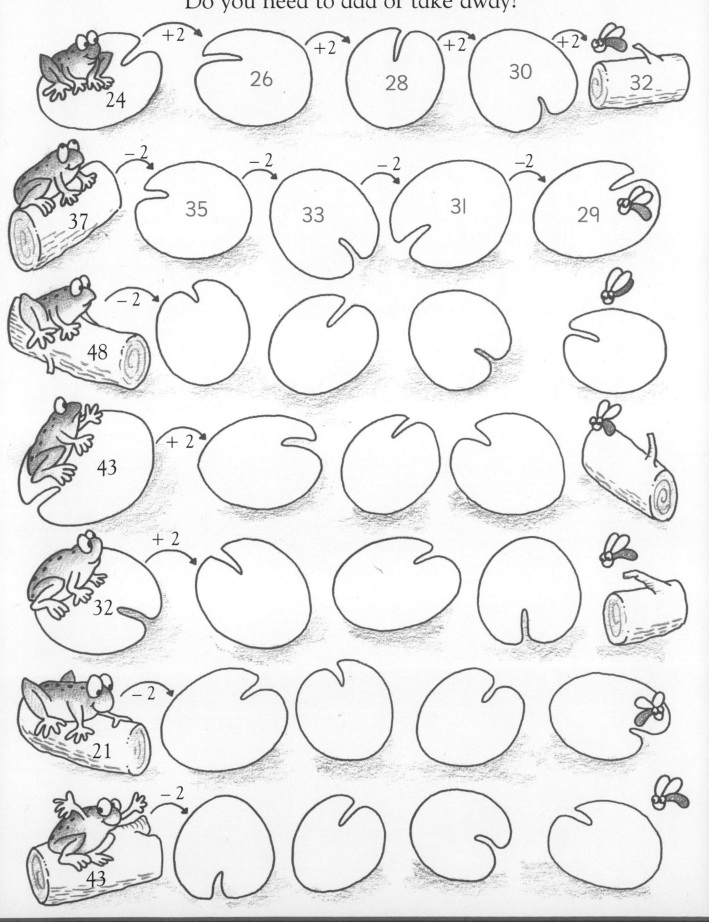

24   +2   26   +2   28   +2   30   +2   32

37   −2   35   −2   33   −2   31   −2   29

48   − 2

43   + 2

32   + 2

21   −2

43   −2

5

Counting in 3s, 4s, and 5s

Draw in the arrows and write the numbers on the toadstools.
Do you need to add or take away?

+3　+3　+3　+3　+3

20　23　26　29　32　35

−3

20

−4

30

−5

26

+4

17

+5

21

Patterns of 2, 5, and 10

Count, colour, and find a pattern.

Count in 2s and colour them red.

1	2	3	4	5	6	7	8	9	10
11	12	13	14	15	16	17	18	19	20
21	22	23	24	25	26	27	28	29	30
31	32	33	34	35	36	37	38	39	40
41	42	43	44	45	46	47	48	49	50

Count in 5s and colour them purple.

1	2	3	4	5	6	7	8	9	10
11	12	13	14	15	16	17	18	19	20
21	22	23	24	25	26	27	28	29	30
31	32	33	34	35	36	37	38	39	40
41	42	43	44	45	46	47	48	49	50

Count in 10s and colour them yellow.

1	2	3	4	5	6	7	8	9	10
11	12	13	14	15	16	17	18	19	20
21	22	23	24	25	26	27	28	29	30
31	32	33	34	35	36	37	38	39	40
41	42	43	44	45	46	47	48	49	50

More or less

Link the spaceships to the planets, and the rockets to the stars.

1 more

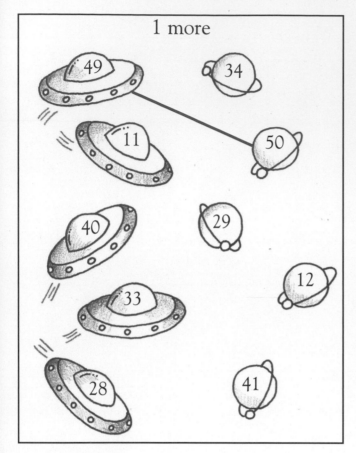

10 more

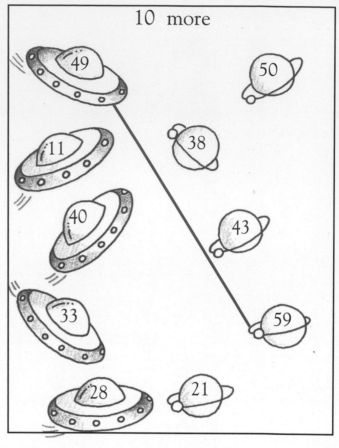

1 less

10 less

Ordering

Write the numbers in order.

smallest first

| 7 | 16 | 26 | | | |

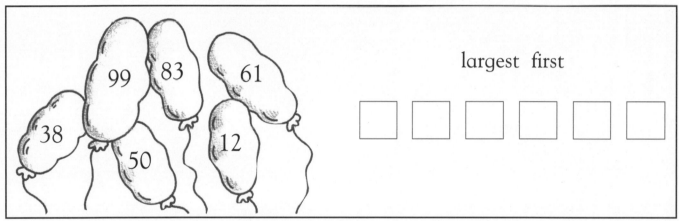

largest first

| | | | | | |

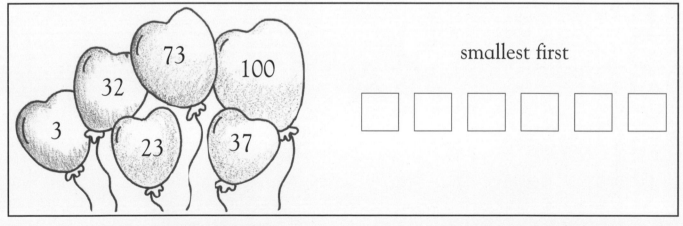

smallest first

| | | | | | |

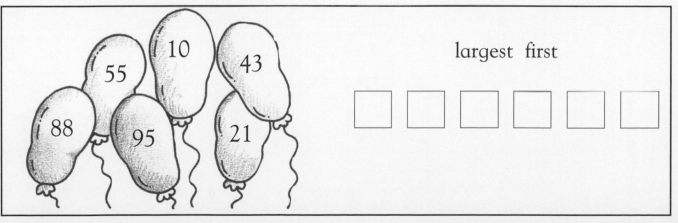

largest first

| | | | | | |

Fractions of shapes

Colour one-third ($\frac{1}{3}$).

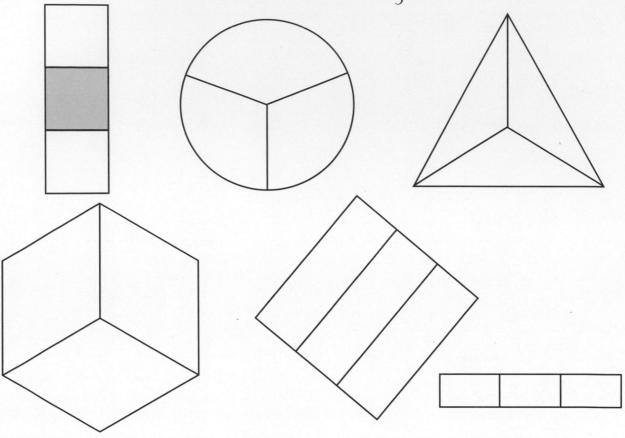

Is it $\frac{1}{3}$? ✓ or ✗.

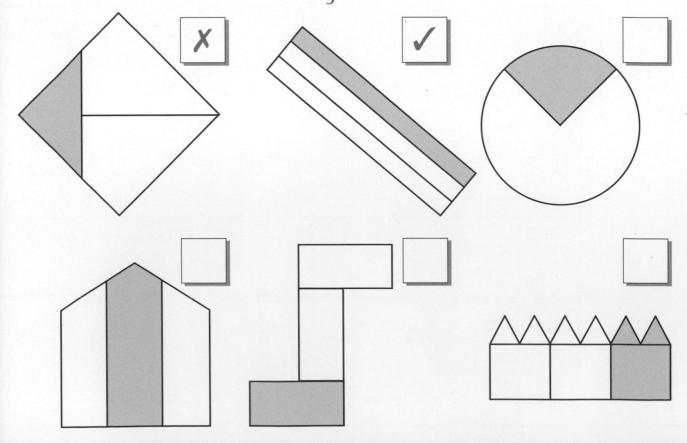

Fractions of numbers

Draw a ring round the objects that make up the fractions and write the missing numbers.

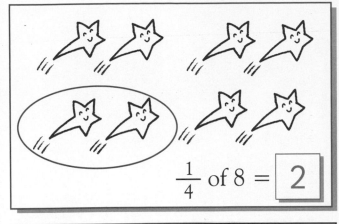

$\frac{1}{4}$ of 8 = 2

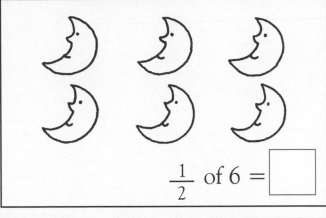

$\frac{1}{2}$ of 6 =

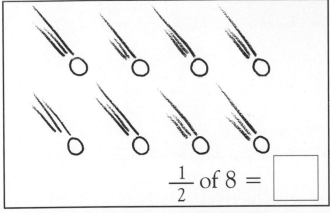

$\frac{1}{2}$ of 8 =

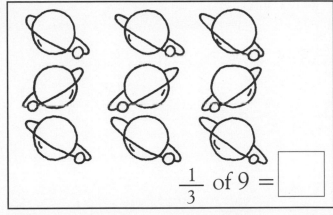

$\frac{1}{3}$ of 9 =

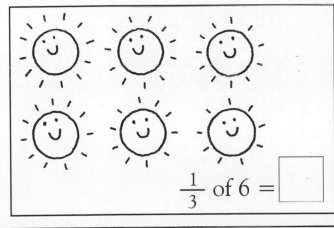

$\frac{1}{3}$ of 6 =

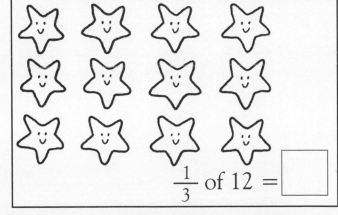

$\frac{1}{3}$ of 12 =

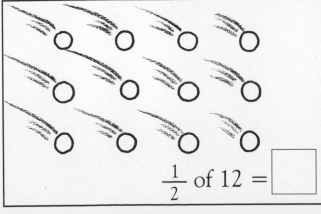

$\frac{1}{2}$ of 12 =

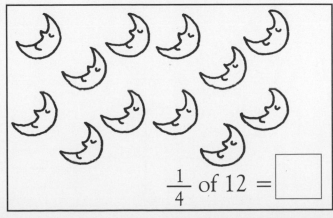

$\frac{1}{4}$ of 12 =

Adding coins

Use three coins each time.
How many different totals can you make?

(5p) + (20p) + (50p) = 75p

(2p) + (1p) + (10p) = 13p

Adding grid

Draw rings round the pairs of numbers that add up to 20.

15	5	3	10	10	4	19
8	6	20	0	9	1	10
12	13	7	12	0	16	1
4	5	10	16	4	5	10
9	2	18	7	20	3	10
11	3	3	1	0	11	9
17	1	1	19	3	18	11

Doubles

Write the missing numbers.

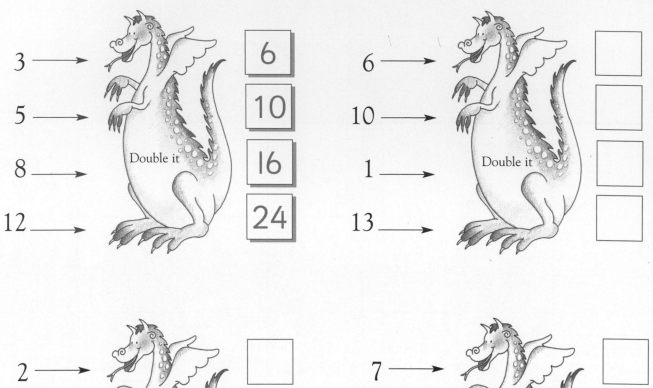

3 → Double it → 6

5 → 10

8 → 16

12 → 24

6 → Double it

10 →

1 →

13 →

2 → Double it

9 →

15 →

4 →

7 → Double it

11 →

14 →

0 →

What has been doubled? Write the missing number.

Double **4** is 8   Double **12** is 24

Double ☐ is 18   Double ☐ is 20   Double ☐ is 14

Double ☐ is 6   Double ☐ is 12   Double ☐ is 10

Double ☐ is 28   Double ☐ is 30

Add and subtract

Use a calculator.

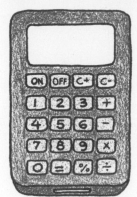

Try out these keys.

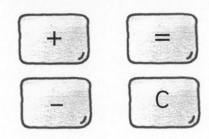

Look at the keys and write the answers.

| 1 | + | 6 | = | **7** |

| 1 | 0 | − | 5 | − | 3 | = | |

| 1 | 9 | − | 9 | = | |

| 1 | 7 | + | 3 | + | 1 | 0 | = | |

| 3 | 0 | − | 1 | 4 | − | 1 | 0 | = | |

| 1 | 2 | + | 1 | 3 | − | 6 | = | |

Is it ✓ or ✗ ? Use the calculator to check.

| 6 | + | 2 | + | 3 | = | 1 | 1 | ✓ |

| 5 | + | 5 | + | 2 | 0 | = | 2 | 5 | ✗ |

| 2 | + | 1 | 2 | + | 4 | = | 2 | 2 | |

| 6 | + | 6 | + | 6 | + | 6 | = | 2 | 4 | |

| 1 | 7 | + | 2 | 3 | = | 3 | 0 | |

| 1 | 9 | + | 1 | 2 | = | 3 | 3 | |

Number wall

Write all the odd numbers. ☐ ☐ ☐

Add them up and write the total. ☐

Write all the even numbers. ☐ ☐ ☐

Add them up and write the total. ☐

Find three numbers which add up to make 13. ☐ ☐ ☐

Write the smallest number. ☐   Double it. ☐

Write the largest number. ☐   Find $\frac{1}{2}$ of it. ☐

Find two ways of making 10. ☐ + ☐ = 10   ☐ + ☐ = 10

Add up all the numbers on the wall. ☐ + ☐ + ☐ + ☐ + ☐ + ☐ = ☐

Answer Section with Parents' Notes

Key Stage 1
Ages 6–7
Beginner

This 8-page section provides answers to all the activities in the book. This will enable you to mark your children's work or can be used by them if they prefer to do their own marking.

The notes for each page help explain the common pitfalls and problems and, where appropriate, give indications as to what practice is needed to ensure your children understand where they have gone wrong.

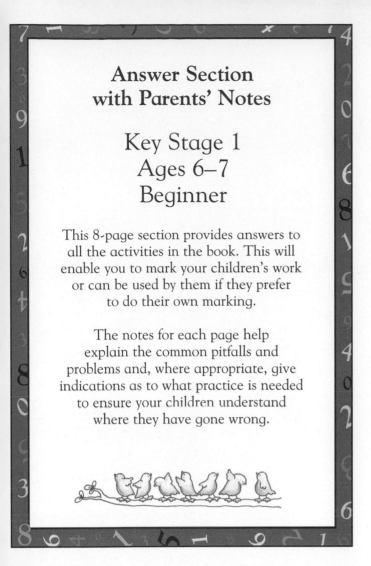

Numbers

Which numbers are the snakes hiding?
Look, and say them as you write.

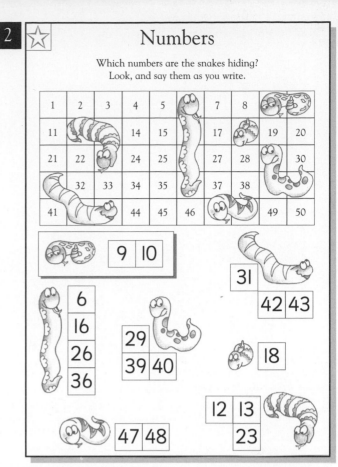

Being able to 'place' numbers in relation to each other is an important skill. Children should be encouraged to look at the patterns in the numbers as they go down columns, as well as across rows. While writing, check whether number formation is being done correctly.

Calculators

Look at the keys on the calculator.
Colour the light bars for each number.

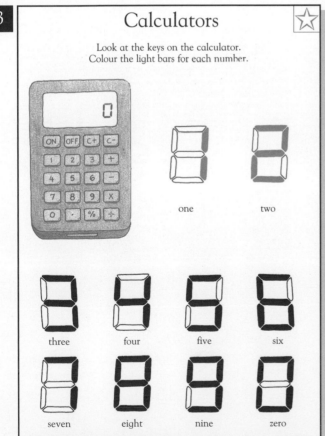

one

two

three

four

five

six

seven

eight

nine

zero

As they compare numbers on light bars with the usual ways of writing, children will realise that both types of number face the same direction and begin in roughly the same place. They can refer to a real calculator if they need more help.

---

1 less or 1 more

Count, draw and write.

Children should choose whether to do '1 more' or '1 less' first. Do they realise that they are taking away (or adding) one each time? Children often find it tricky when numbers 'cross a ten', e.g. 79. Practice with small numbers will help.

Counting in 2s

Draw in the hops and write in the numbers.
Do you need to add or take away?

24 →+2→ 26 →+2→ 28 →+2→ 30 →+2→ 32

37 →−2→ 35 →−2→ 33 →−2→ 31 →−2→ 29

48 →−2→ 46 44 42 40

43 →+2→ 45 47 49 51

32 →+2→ 34 36 38 40

21 →−2→ 19 17 15 13

43 →−2→ 41 39 37 35

Children should realise that when adding or taking away two, if they begin with an odd number they will end with an odd number, and vice versa. They can use this information to check their answers and to help them add or subtract two from any other number.

Counting in 3s, 4s, and 5s

Draw in the arrows and write the numbers on the toadstools.
Do you need to add or take away?

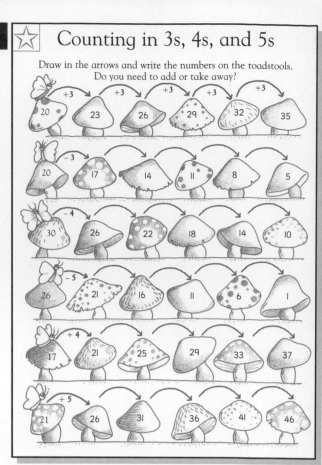

20 →+3→ 23 →+3→ 26 →+3→ 29 →+3→ 32 →+3→ 35

20 →−3→ 17 14 11 8 5

30 →−4→ 26 22 18 14 10

26 →−5→ 21 16 11 6 1

17 →+4→ 21 25 29 33 37

21 →+5→ 26 31 36 41 46

Can children now 'picture' 3 more, or 4 less, in their minds without fingers or other aids? Try to help them realise that +3 is the opposite of −3. Having moved from 20 to 5 in steps of 3, can they get back to 20 again? (They need to +3 the same number of times.)

Patterns of 2, 5, and 10

Count, colour, and find a pattern.

Count in 2s and colour them red.

1	2	3	4	5	6	7	8	9	10
11	12	13	14	15	16	17	18	19	20
21	22	23	24	25	26	27	28	29	30
31	32	33	34	35	36	37	38	39	40
41	42	43	44	45	46	47	48	49	50

Count in 5s and colour them purple.

1	2	3	4	5	6	7	8	9	10
11	12	13	14	15	16	17	18	19	20
21	22	23	24	25	26	27	28	29	30
31	32	33	34	35	36	37	38	39	40
41	42	43	44	45	46	47	48	49	50

Count in 10s and colour them yellow.

1	2	3	4	5	6	7	8	9	10
11	12	13	14	15	16	17	18	19	20
21	22	23	24	25	26	27	28	29	30
31	32	33	34	35	36	37	38	39	40
41	42	43	44	45	46	47	48	49	50

Discuss the patterns made. Are there any numbers that are coloured in all the patterns? (The 10s will be.) Why is this? Help children see that all the multiples of 5 end in a 5 or a 0.

More or less

Link the spaceships to the planets, and the rockets to the stars.

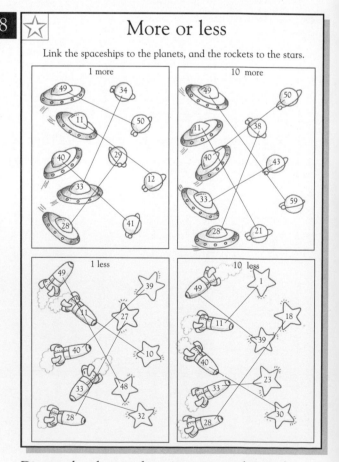

1 more

10 more

1 less

10 less

Discuss the changes happening to each set of numbers. Is it the tens or the units digit that changes? Is 'ten more' the same as adding or taking away 10? Do the numbers always get larger or smaller when finding '10 less'?

Ordering

Write the numbers in order.

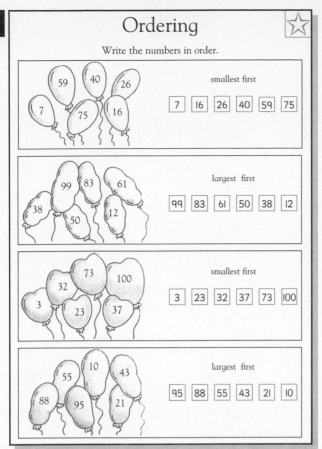

Beware of possible reversals such as reading 16 as 61. This indicates a need for more work on place values. In the 3rd section, 23, 32, 37, and 73 have been included to highlight this. Can the children explain the different 'values' of the threes in 37 and 73?

Fractions of shapes

Colour one-third $\left(\frac{1}{3}\right)$.

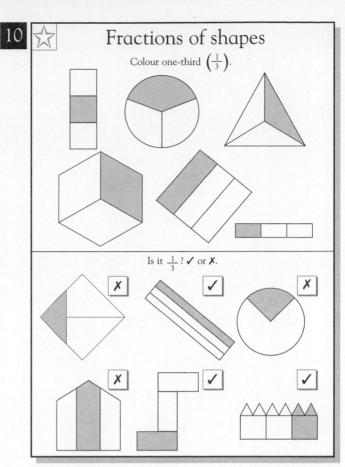

Is it $\frac{1}{3}$? ✓ or ✗.

Explain why some of the pictures in the second section do not have 'one-third' coloured in, even though each shape is cut into three pieces. (The pieces are not all of equal size.) As an extra activity, can the children name any of the shapes they see on the page?

Fractions of numbers

Draw a ring round the objects that make up the fractions and write the missing numbers.

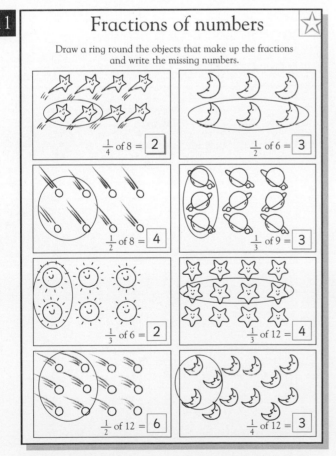

$\frac{1}{4}$ of 8 = 2

$\frac{1}{2}$ of 6 = 3

$\frac{1}{2}$ of 8 = 4

$\frac{1}{3}$ of 9 = 3

$\frac{1}{3}$ of 6 = 2

$\frac{1}{3}$ of 12 = 4

$\frac{1}{2}$ of 12 = 6

$\frac{1}{4}$ of 12 = 3

Children should look at the bottom number of the fraction (denominator) to check how many groups the set should be split into. ($\frac{1}{3}$ will need three groups.) You can try extending to questions like 'if one-third of the stars is 4, how many would be in two-thirds?'

Adding coins

Use three coins each time.
How many different totals can you make?

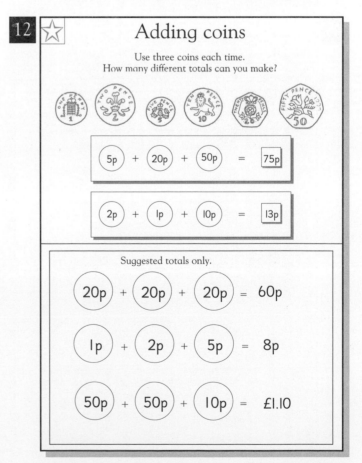

5p + 20p + 50p = 75p

2p + 1p + 10p = 13p

Suggested totals only.

20p + 20p + 20p = 60p

1p + 2p + 5p = 8p

50p + 50p + 10p = £1.10

If children find adding the 50p and 20p coins difficult, cover them up, and do the same activity with only the lower value coins. Do they prefer to add up the tens first and then count on the units? Discuss their methods and let them tackle things in their preferred way.

Adding grid

Draw rings round the pairs of numbers that add up to 20.

15	5	3	10	10	4	19
8	6	20	0	9	1	10
12	13	7	12	0	16	1
4	5	10	16	4	5	10
9	2	18	7	20	3	10
11	3	3	1	0	11	9
17	1	1	19	3	18	11

If children find this page difficult, it would be worth finding 20 objects, such as pencils or pasta shapes, and finding different ways of splitting them into 2 piles, e.g. 2 and 18, 15 and 5. Children can then look for these pairs of numbers.

Doubles

Write the missing numbers.

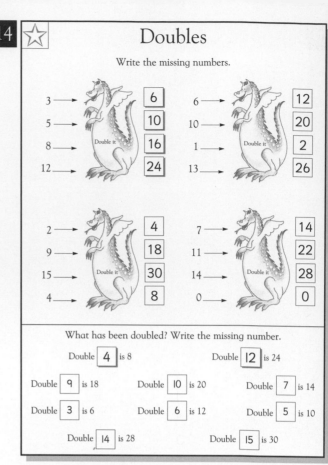

3 →	6
5 →	10
8 →	16
12 →	24

6 →	12
10 →	20
1 →	2
13 →	26

2 →	4
9 →	18
15 →	30
4 →	8

7 →	14
11 →	22
14 →	28
0 →	0

What has been doubled? Write the missing number.

Double 4 is 8   Double 12 is 24

Double 9 is 18   Double 10 is 20   Double 7 is 14

Double 3 is 6   Double 6 is 12   Double 5 is 10

Double 14 is 28   Double 15 is 30

Explain that 'doubling' is the same as adding two lots of the same number together. If children cannot yet double in their heads, use pasta shapes to make two piles of the number and add them up; this helps with initial calculations. Children should aim to memorise the answers.

Add and subtract

Use a calculator.   Try out these keys.

$+$ $=$

$-$ C

Look at the keys and write the answers.

1 + 6 = **7**

1 0 − 5 − 3 = **2**

1 9 − 9 = **10**

1 7 + 3 + 1 0 = **30**

3 0 − 1 4 − 1 0 = **6**

1 2 + 1 3 − 6 = **19**

Is it ✓ or ✗ ? Use the calculator to check.

6 + 2 + 3 = 1 1 ✓

5 + 5 + 2 0 = 2 5 ✗

2 + 1 2 + 4 = 2 2 ✗

6 + 6 + 6 + 6 = 2 4 ✓

1 7 + 2 3 = 3 0 ✗

1 9 + 1 2 = 3 3 ✗

This page is a way of revising addition and subtraction, while simultaneously familiarising the children with calculators.

Number wall

Write all the odd numbers. 3 5 7

Add them up and write the total. 15

Write all the even numbers. 4 6 8

Add them up and write the total. 18

Find three numbers which add up to make 13. 6 + 4 + 3

Write the smallest number. 3   Double it. 6

Write the largest number. 8   Find $\frac{1}{2}$ of it. 4

Find two ways of making 10. 6 + 4 =10   7 + 3 =10

Add up all the numbers on the wall. 6 + 5 + 8 + 3 + 4 + 7 = 33

Children may need help reading the questions. Make them look for 'easy options': when adding the even numbers they may recognise that 4 and 6 make 10, to which 8 can then be added . Can they recognise other such addition pairs, without counting on?

Multiplying by 2

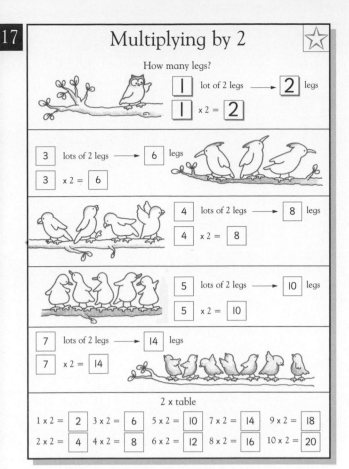

How many legs?

1 lot of 2 legs → 2 legs
1 x 2 = 2

3 lots of 2 legs → 6 legs
3 x 2 = 6

4 lots of 2 legs → 8 legs
4 x 2 = 8

5 lots of 2 legs → 10 legs
5 x 2 = 10

7 lots of 2 legs → 14 legs
7 x 2 = 14

2 x table

1 x 2 = 2	3 x 2 = 6	5 x 2 = 10	7 x 2 = 14	9 x 2 = 18
2 x 2 = 4	4 x 2 = 8	6 x 2 = 12	8 x 2 = 16	10 x 2 = 20

Can children see the pattern created by the units digits? They follow 2, 4, 6, 8, 0. Do they know whether these are odd or even numbers? Reciting 2, 4, 6, 8, 10 is easy but can they give you a fast response if you ask them questions like, 'What are 3 lots of 2'?

Multiplying by 10

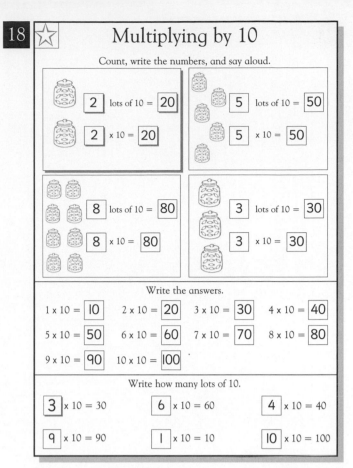

Count, write the numbers, and say aloud.

2 lots of 10 = 20
2 x 10 = 20

5 lots of 10 = 50
5 x 10 = 50

8 lots of 10 = 80
8 x 10 = 80

3 lots of 10 = 30
3 x 10 = 30

Write the answers.

1 x 10 = 10   2 x 10 = 20   3 x 10 = 30   4 x 10 = 40
5 x 10 = 50   6 x 10 = 60   7 x 10 = 70   8 x 10 = 80
9 x 10 = 90   10 x 10 = 100

Write how many lots of 10.

3 x 10 = 30   6 x 10 = 60   4 x 10 = 40
9 x 10 = 90   1 x 10 = 10   10 x 10 = 100

Whatever word children have learnt for multiplication, they should realise that it means 'lots of'. Reinforce the idea that multiplying by a number is really adding that many lots of the number together. 4 x10 is the same as 4 lots of 10, and 10+10+10+10.

Multiplying by 5

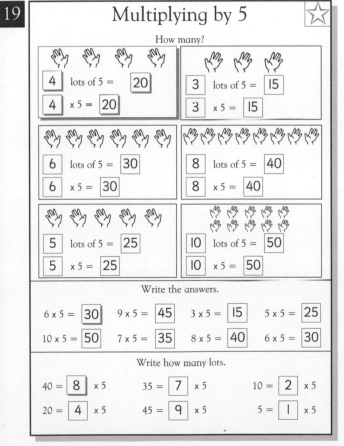

How many?

4 lots of 5 = 20
4 x 5 = 20

3 lots of 5 = 15
3 x 5 = 15

6 lots of 5 = 30
6 x 5 = 30

8 lots of 5 = 40
8 x 5 = 40

5 lots of 5 = 25
5 x 5 = 25

10 lots of 5 = 50
10 x 5 = 50

Write the answers.

6 x 5 = 30   9 x 5 = 45   3 x 5 = 15   5 x 5 = 25
10 x 5 = 50   7 x 5 = 35   8 x 5 = 40   6 x 5 = 30

Write how many lots.

40 = 8 x 5   35 = 7 x 5   10 = 2 x 5
20 = 4 x 5   45 = 9 x 5   5 = 1 x 5

Children should remember that the answers in the 5x table always end in 0 or 5. They can use this fact to check their own work to make sure that they do not include any answers that do not fit this rule. Can they also use this to write out the 5x table?

Real life problems

All the piggy banks need 20p. Draw different coins in each one. You can use any coin more than once.

Explain that to make 5p, five 1p coins or 2p, 2p, 1p, or 2p, 1p, 1p, 1p, or a 5p coin on its own can be used. So 10p can be made with any of these combinations plus a 5p coin, then another 10p coin will make 20p.

Real life problems

Draw the stamps on the letters.
You can use any stamp more than once.

Heather Hedgehog
1 The Leaf Pile
Snowdrop Corner
Gardenshire
12p

Doctor Dilly Dinosaur
6 The Swamp
Mud Town
20p

Master Robbie Robot
999 Mechanical Mansion
Metalville
21p

Cheeky Charlie Chimp
100 Banana Court
Giggleworthy
Apeshire
18p

Mr Bertie Bear
The Toy Box
Barry's Bedroom
The Big House
11p

Sir Samuel Spider
Wonder Web
Grandad's Greenhouse
Gardensbottom
25p

Children may use different stamp combinations to reach the totals. However, in life we would use as few stamps as possible, so they would benefit from trying to reduce the number on any envelope. For 6p, 5p and 1p would be better than six 1p stamps.

Subtraction tables

Finish each table.

−	2	3	5	10
11	9	8	6	1
15	13	12	10	5
20	18	17	15	10

−	1	6	8	9
14	13	8	6	5
19	18	13	11	10
25	24	19	17	16

−	0	4	7	11
12	12	8	5	1
28	28	24	21	17
30	30	26	23	19

Start by asking children to point out on the table where the information is, and where the answer goes. If they find this difficult, try 'sliding' pencils along, one from each of the numbers being used, and letting them meet in the space where the answer should go.

Counting down

The rocket can only lift off at zero.
Use take aways to get back to 0 in 4 moves.

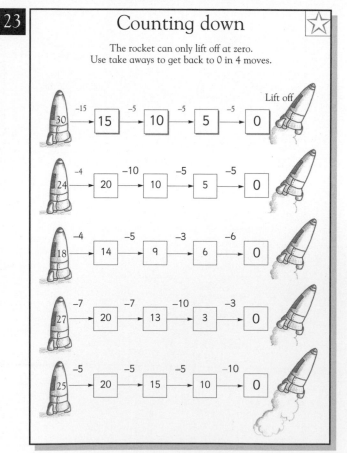

Lift off

There are many possible answers. If children reach zero too soon, can they split one of their own numbers into two smaller ones and take each away separately? If they can't reach zero, can they add the number they have left to an earlier one and take all of it away in one go?

Clocks

Write the times under the clocks.

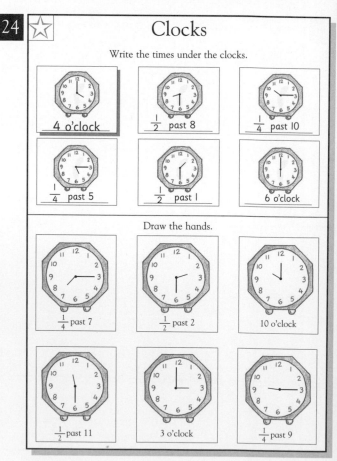

4 o'clock

$\frac{1}{2}$ past 8

$\frac{1}{4}$ past 10

$\frac{1}{4}$ past 5

$\frac{1}{2}$ past 1

6 o'clock

Draw the hands.

$\frac{1}{4}$ past 7

$\frac{1}{2}$ past 2

10 o'clock

$\frac{1}{2}$ past 11

3 o'clock

$\frac{1}{4}$ past 9

The length of the clock hands is important to ensure that times such as half past 12 and 6 o'clock are not confused. Talk about the shape made from 12 o'clock to $\frac{1}{4}$ past or $\frac{1}{2}$ past. Can they relate this to $\frac{1}{4}$ or $\frac{1}{2}$ of a circle?

Digital clocks

Write the times under the clocks.

12:15	**6:00**	**9:00**
¼ past 12	6 o'clock	9 o'clock
10:30	**8:30**	**5:15**
½ past 10	½ past 8	¼ past 5

Fill in the digital times on the clock faces.

11:30	**1:30**	**12:00**
½ past 11	½ past 1	12 o'clock
3:15	**8:00**	**10:15**
¼ past 3	8 o'clock	¼ past 10

Watch out for confusion between the digital versions of 5 and 2. It is worthwhile comparing them with traditional numbers to see their similarities and differences. Children should see that the start positions of both digital and traditional numbers are the same.

Match the times

Draw a line to link the matching times.

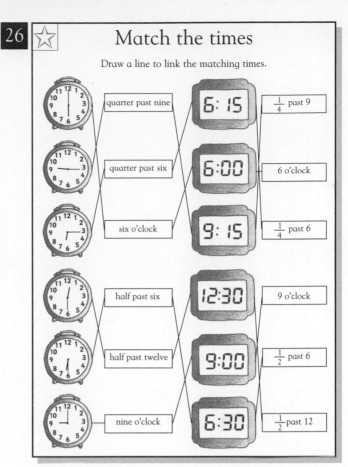

quarter past nine — 6:15 — ¼ past 9
quarter past six — 6:00 — 6 o'clock
six o'clock — 9:15 — ¼ past 6

half past six — 12:30 — 9 o'clock
half past twelve — 9:00 — ½ past 6
nine o'clock — 6:30 — ½ past 12

Can children find examples of both digital and analogue times around the home, such as the video or television? Can they draw both types of clock to show the time they finish school? Talk about other ways of measuring time such as sand-timers or sundials.

Do you know?

Put the months in order by writing a number on each page.

September 9th, April 4th, February 2nd, August 8th, May 5th, March 3rd, December 12th, June 6th, November 11th, January 1st, October 10th, July 7th

How many...

... seconds in a minute?	60	... minutes in an hour?	60
... hours in a day?	24	... days in a week?	7
... days in a year?	365	... months in a year?	12

Learn this rhyme.

30 days have September,
April, June, and November.
All the rest have 31,
Except February alone
That has 28 days clear
29 in each leap year.

How many days are there in your birthday month?

These numbers are all facts that have to be learned rather than 'found out'. Children can learn the rhyme and then have fun answering questions about the number of days in 'the month Christmas is in' or 'the month we start a new school year'.

Going shopping

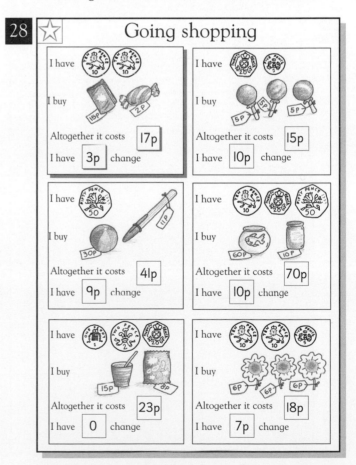

I have | I buy 15p 2p | Altogether it costs 17p | I have 3p change

I have | I buy 5p 5p | Altogether it costs 15p | I have 10p change

I have | I buy 30p 11p | Altogether it costs 41p | I have 9p change

I have | I buy 60p 10p | Altogether it costs 70p | I have 10p change

I have | I buy 15p 8p | Altogether it costs 23p | I have 0 change

I have | I buy 6p 6p 6p | Altogether it costs 18p | I have 7p change

Though some numbers look large, the sums are easy, as they involve whole tens. Children should realise that 'change' is the difference between what they spend and what they have to start with. They may either count on from the cost to the amount left, or vice versa.

Venn diagrams ⭐

Flowers with red petals   Flowers with white petals

How many flowers …

… with red petals? **7** … with white petals? **10** … with both red <u>and</u> white petals? **2**

Shapes with straight sides   Shapes with curved sides

How many shapes …

… with straight sides? **8** … with curved sides? **6** … with straight <u>and</u> curved sides? **3**

Odd numbers   Numbers more than ten

5
3
1
9 11 19 12 16
7 20 14

How many numbers are …

… odd? **7** … more than ten? **6** … odd <u>and</u> more than ten? **2**

Can children explain why some of the pictures or numbers are in the overlapping part of the two circles? They must remember that these numbers should be included while counting either of the main sets. Draw other flowers or shapes and ask where to include them.

⭐ Carroll diagrams

	legs	no legs
green		
not green		

How many creatures are…

… green with no legs **2**

… not green **7**

… not green with legs **3**

… not green with no legs **4**

	Shapes that have 4 sides	Shapes that do <u>not</u> have 4 sides
white		
green		

How many shapes are…

… white **9**

… green with 4 sides **5**

…white but do <u>not</u> have 4 sides **6**

… green but do <u>not</u> have 4 sides **6**

	less than 6	more than 6
odd	1 3 5	7 9 11
even	2 4	8 10 12

How many numbers are…

… odd **6**

… odd and more than 6 **3**

… even and more than 6 **3**

… less than 6 **5**

The most frequently made errors with these diagrams occur when children do not look right down a column or right across a row when counting. Discuss with children issues like where all creatures with legs are drawn and why they are not all in the same box.

2D Shapes ⭐

Add up the shapes to find out how much each picture will cost.

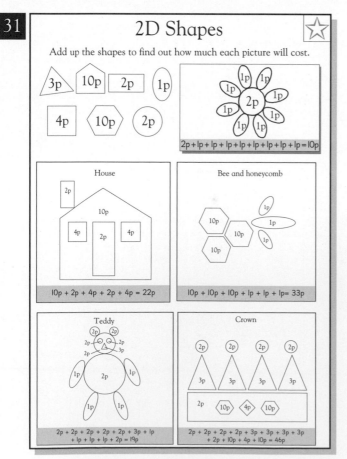

3p 10p 2p 1p

4p 10p 2p

2p + 1p + 1p + 1p + 1p + 1p + 1p + 1p + 1p = 10p

House

2p
10p
4p 2p 4p

10p + 2p + 4p + 2p + 4p = 22p

Bee and honeycomb

10p + 10p + 10p + 1p + 1p + 1p = 33p

Teddy

2p + 2p + 2p + 2p + 2p + 3p + 1p + 1p + 1p + 1p + 2p = 19p

Crown

2p + 2p + 2p + 2p + 3p + 3p + 3p + 3p + 2p + 10p + 4p + 10p = 46p

Encourage children to find their own ways of making the adding up easier. If they find adding difficult, help them to use counters to count out the individual amounts and then to total these up.

⭐ 3D Shapes

Label the 3D shapes.
(cone, cylinder, pyramid, cube, sphere, cuboid)

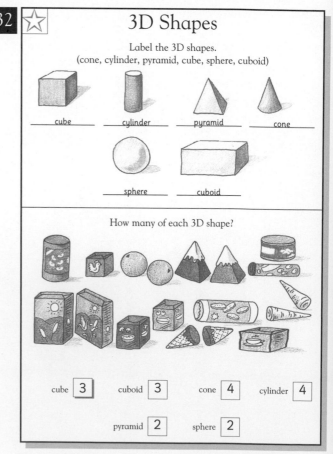

cube   cylinder   pyramid   cone

sphere   cuboid

How many of each 3D shape?

cube **3**   cuboid **3**   cone **4**   cylinder **4**

pyramid **2**   sphere **2**

Can children describe the differences between a cube and a cuboid, or a cone and a cylinder? They should be beginning to use appropriate mathematical language such as curved, straight, corners, sides etc.

Multiplying by 2

How many legs?

 lot of 2 legs ⟶ **2** legs

 x 2 = **2**

---

 lots of 2 legs ⟶ ☐ legs

 x 2 = ☐

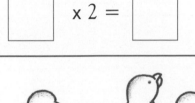

 lots of 2 legs ⟶ ☐ legs

 x 2 = ☐

 lots of 2 legs ⟶ ☐ legs

 x 2 = ☐

---

 lots of 2 legs ⟶ ☐ legs

 x 2 = ☐

---

2 x table

1 x 2 = ☐	3 x 2 = ☐	5 x 2 = ☐	7 x 2 = ☐	9 x 2 = ☐
2 x 2 = ☐	4 x 2 = ☐	6 x 2 = ☐	8 x 2 = ☐	10 x 2 = ☐

Multiplying by 10

Count, write the numbers, and say aloud.

 2 lots of 10 = **20**

 2 x 10 = **20**

 [ ] lots of 10 = [ ]

 [ ] x 10 = [ ]

 [ ] lots of 10 = [ ]

[ ] x 10 = [ ]

 [ ] lots of 10 = [ ]

[ ] x 10 = [ ]

Write the answers.

1 x 10 = [ ]   2 x 10 = [ ]   3 x 10 = [ ]   4 x 10 = [ ]

5 x 10 = [ ]   6 x 10 = [ ]   7 x 10 = [ ]   8 x 10 = [ ]

9 x 10 = [ ]   10 x 10 = [ ]

Write how many lots of 10.

3 x 10 = 30   [ ] x 10 = 60   [ ] x 10 = 40

[ ] x 10 = 90   [ ] x 10 = 10   [ ] x 10 = 100

Multiplying by 5

How many?

| 4 | lots of 5 = | 20 |

| 4 | x 5 = | 20 |

☐ lots of 5 = ☐

☐ x 5 = ☐

☐ lots of 5 = ☐

☐ x 5 = ☐

☐ lots of 5 = ☐

☐ x 5 = ☐

☐ lots of 5 = ☐

☐ x 5 = ☐

☐ lots of 5 = ☐

☐ x 5 = ☐

Write the answers.

6 x 5 = 30   9 x 5 = ☐   3 x 5 = ☐   5 x 5 = ☐

10 x 5 = ☐   7 x 5 = ☐   8 x 5 = ☐   6 x 5 = ☐

Write how many lots.

40 = 8 x 5   35 = ☐ x 5   10 = ☐ x 5

20 = ☐ x 5   45 = ☐ x 5   5 = ☐ x 5

Real life problems

All the piggy banks need 20p. Draw different coins in each one.
You can use any coin more than once.

Real life problems

 6p 5p 4p 2p 1p

Draw the stamps on the letters.
You can use any stamp more than once.

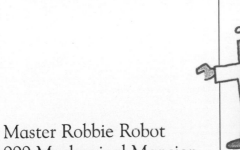

Heather Hedgehog
1 The Leaf Pile
Snowdrop Corner
Gardenshire

12p

Doctor Dilly Dinosaur
6 The Swamp
Mud Town

20p

Master Robbie Robot
999 Mechanical Mansion
Metalville

21p

Cheeky Charlie Chimp
100 Banana Court
Giggleworthy
Apeshire

18p

Mr Bertie Bear
The Toy Box
Barry's Bedroom
The Big House

11p

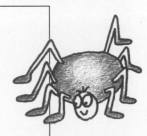

Sir Samuel Spider
Wonder Web
Grandad's Greenhouse
Gardensbottom

25p

Subtraction tables

Finish each table.

−	2	3	5	10
11	9	8		
15	13			
20				

−	1	6	8	9
14				
19	18	13	11	
25				

−	0	4	7	11
12			5	
28			21	
30				

Counting down

The rocket can only lift off at zero.
Use take aways to get back to 0 in 4 moves.

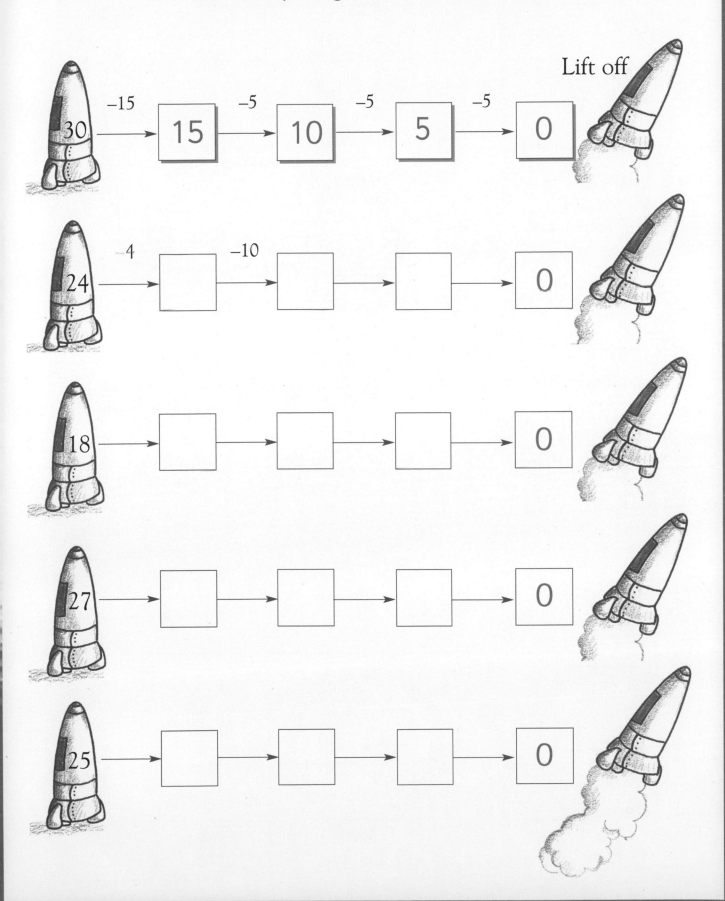

Lift off

	−15		−5		−5		−5	
30		15		10		5		0

	−4		−10					
24								0

| 18 | | | | | | | | 0 |

| 27 | | | | | | | | 0 |

| 25 | | | | | | | | 0 |

Clocks

Write the times under the clocks.

4 o'clock

Draw the hands.

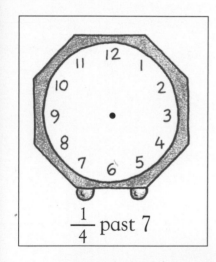

$\frac{1}{4}$ past 7

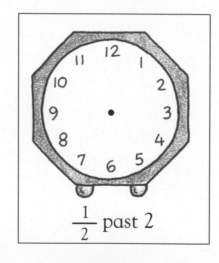

$\frac{1}{2}$ past 2

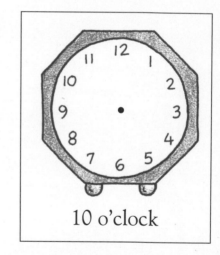

10 o'clock

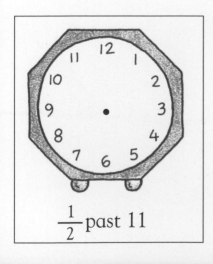

$\frac{1}{2}$ past 11

3 o'clock

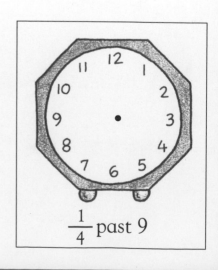

$\frac{1}{4}$ past 9

Digital clocks

Write the times under the clocks.

$\frac{1}{4}$ past 12

Fill in the digital times on the clock faces.

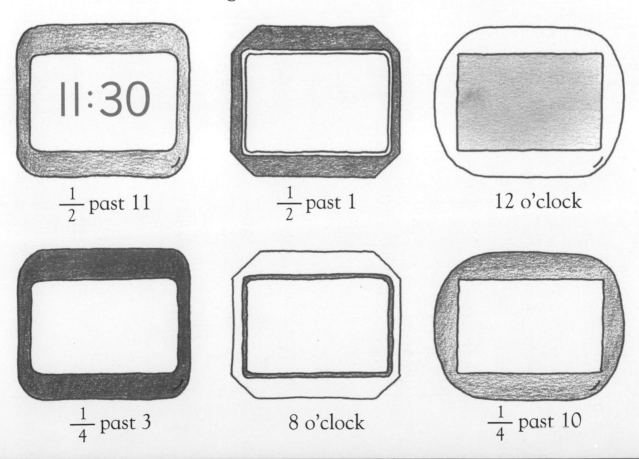

$\frac{1}{2}$ past 11 $\frac{1}{2}$ past 1   12 o'clock

$\frac{1}{4}$ past 3   8 o'clock $\frac{1}{4}$ past 10

Match the times

Draw a line to link the matching times.

quarter past nine

6: 15

$\frac{1}{4}$ past 9

quarter past six

6:00

6 o'clock

six o'clock

9: 15

$\frac{1}{4}$ past 6

half past six

12:30

9 o'clock

half past twelve

9:00

$\frac{1}{2}$ past 6

nine o'clock

6:30

$\frac{1}{2}$ past 12

Do you know?

Put the months in order by writing a number on each page.

How many...

... seconds in a minute? ☐   ... minutes in an hour? ☐

... hours in a day? ☐   ... days in a week? ☐

... days in a year? ☐   ... months in a year? ☐

Learn this rhyme.

30 days have September,
April, June, and November.
All the rest have 31,
Except February alone
That has 28 days clear
29 in each leap year.

How many days are there in your birthday month? ☐

Going shopping

I have

I buy

Altogether it costs **17p**

I have **3p** change

I have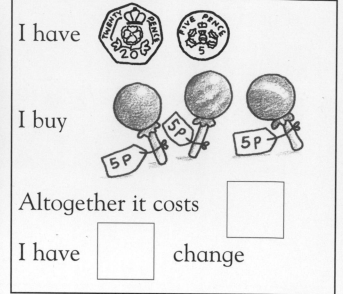

I buy

Altogether it costs ☐

I have ☐ change

I have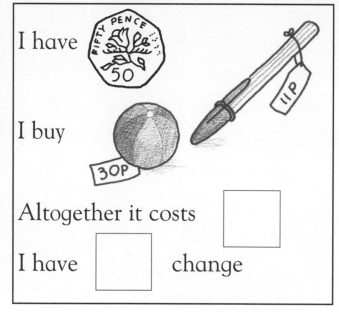

I buy

Altogether it costs ☐

I have ☐ change

I have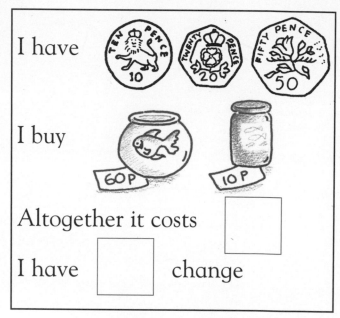

I buy

Altogether it costs ☐

I have ☐ change

I have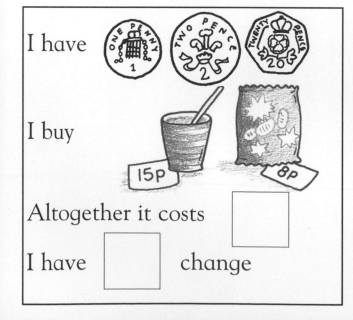

I buy

Altogether it costs ☐

I have ☐ change

I have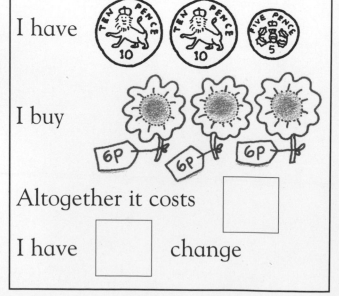

I buy

Altogether it costs ☐

I have ☐ change

Venn diagrams

Flowers with red petals   Flowers with white petals

How many flowers ...

... with red petals? $\boxed{7}$ ... with white petals? $\boxed{10}$ ... with both red and white petals? $\boxed{2}$

Shapes with straight sides   Shapes with curved sides

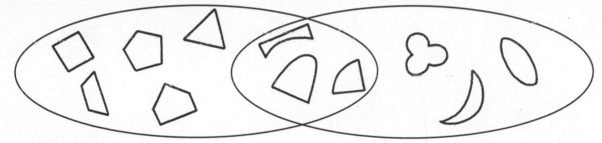

How many shapes ...

... with straight sides? $\boxed{}$ ... with curved sides? $\boxed{}$ ... with straight and curved sides? $\boxed{}$

Odd numbers   Numbers more than ten

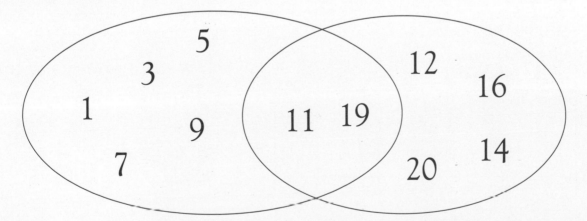

How many numbers are ...

... odd? $\boxed{}$ ... more than ten? $\boxed{}$ ... odd and more than ten? $\boxed{}$

Carroll diagrams

	legs	no legs
green		
not green		

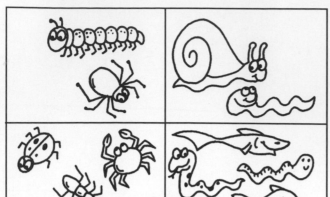

How many creatures are...

... green with no legs **2**

... not green **7**

... not green with legs **3**

... not green with no legs **4**

	Shapes that have 4 sides	Shapes that do not have 4 sides
white		
green		

How many shapes are...

... white

... green with 4 sides

...white but do not have 4 sides

... green but do not have 4 sides

	less than 6	more than 6
odd	1 3 5	7 9 11
even	2 4	8 10 12

How many numbers are...

... odd

... odd and more than 6

... even and more than 6

... less than 6

30

2D Shapes

Add up the shapes to find out how much each picture will cost.

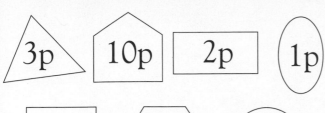

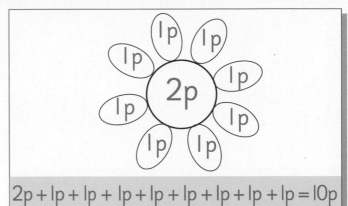

$2p + 1p + 1p + 1p + 1p + 1p + 1p + 1p + 1p = 10p$

House

Bee and honeycomb

Teddy

Crown

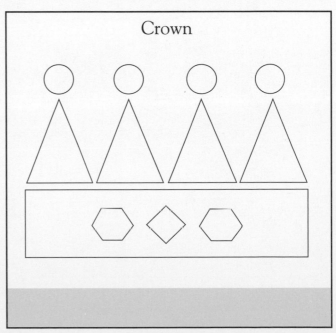

3D Shapes

Label the 3D shapes.
(cone, cylinder, pyramid, cube, sphere, cuboid)

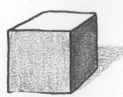 

cube _____   _____   _____   _____

 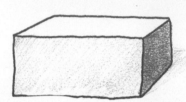

_____   _____

How many of each 3D shape?

cube [3]   cuboid [ ]   cone [ ]   cylinder [ ]

pyramid [ ]   sphere [ ]